# The CLARA BARTON
## You Never Knew

BY JAMES LINCOLN COLLIER

W.M. Allison

Children's Press®
A Division of Scholastic Inc.
New York Toronto London Auckland Sydney
Mexico City New Delhi Hong Kong
Danbury, Connecticut

Library of Congress Cataloging-in-Publication Data

Collier, James Lincoln, 1928-
  The Clara Barton you never knew / by James Lincoln Collier;
[illustrations by Greg Copeland].
        p. cm.
Summary: Explores the childhood, character, and influential events that
shaped the life of the Civil War nurse who went on to found the American
Red Cross.
Includes bibliographical references and index.
  ISBN 0-516-24346-2  (lib. bdg.)        0-516-25838-9 (pbk.)
  1.  Barton, Clara, 1821-1912—Juvenile literature. 2.  Red Cross—United
States—Biography—Juvenile literature. 3.  Nurses—United States—
Biography—Juvenile literature. [1. Barton, Clara, 1821-1912. 2. Nurses.
3. American National Red Cross. 4. Women—Biography.]  I. Copeland,
Greg, ill. II. Title.
  HV569.B3C645 2003
  361.7'634'092—dc21

                                2003005250

Illustrations by Greg Copeland
Book design by A. Natacha Pimentel C.

Photographs © 2003: Art Resource, NY/Fine Art Photographic Library,
London/Galerie Mensing: 12; Bridgeman Art Library International Ltd.,
London/New York/Ivanovo Museum of Art, Ivanovo, Russia,: 61; Clara
Barton Birthplace Museum, North Oxford, MA: 7 left, 7 right, 14, 15, 18;
Clara Barton National Historic Site/National Park Service, Glen Echo,
MD: cover, 4; Corbis Images: 26, 31, 39, 73 (Bettmann), 48 (Medford
Historical Society Collection), 64 (Swim Ink), 30, 46, 50, 68, 74;
International Federation of the Red Cross: 58; Library of Congress: 1,
8, 24, 36, 54; North Wind Picture Archives: 6, 21, 28, 32, 33, 59, 71.

# CONTENTS

CHAPTER 1
The Shy Tomboy . . . . . . . . . . . . . . . . . . . . . .5

CHAPTER 2
Trying to Find Her Way . . . . . . . . . . . . . . . . .19

CHAPTER 3
The Angel of the Battlefield . . . . . . . . . . . . . . .37

CHAPTER 4
Looking for a New Life . . . . . . . . . . . . . . . . . .51

CHAPTER 5
Founding the American Red Cross . . . . . . . . . . . .65

Map . . . . . . . . . . . . . . . . . . . . . . . . . . . . . .76

Author's Note on Sources . . . . . . . . . . . . . . . . .77

Index . . . . . . . . . . . . . . . . . . . . . . . . . . . . .78

# Chapter 1

# THE SHY TOMBOY

FROM CHILDHOOD, CLARA BARTON WAS different. All of her life she would be shy. As a child, she would go out in freezing weather without her gloves because she was too timid to ask her parents for a new pair. As an adult, she would suffer intensely from stage fright when she had to give a talk. Long after she had become one of the most famous women in America she said, "To this day I would rather stand behind the lines of artillery at Antietam or cross the pontoon bridge under fire at Fredericksburg than to be expected to preside at a public meeting."

*Clara Barton, photographed in the 1880s. She gave much of her life to helping others.*

And yet this shy, even timid woman had no problem marching up to presidents, kings, and emperors demanding that they help her in her projects. She had no fear of rushing onto a battlefield to bandage wounded men. And almost by herself, she created the American Red Cross, today one of the nation's most important voluntary organizations. Few Americans of her time accomplished more than Clara Barton. How could this shy woman have done so much great work?

Clara Barton was born on Christmas Day in the little town of North Oxford, Massachusetts, about forty miles west of Boston. The year was 1821. She was named for an aunt, who in turn had been named for the heroine of a very popular novel of the mid-1700s named Clarissa Harlowe. As a girl, Clarissa Harlowe Barton shortened her name to Clara, and she would be known as Clara Barton for the rest of her life.

Late in life, when she was an old woman, Clara wrote a little book about her childhood. She made her life as a girl seem quite pleasant. And in many ways it was. But there was a dark side to it, too, for her mother and father fought a good deal. Her mother was particularly difficult. To her credit, however, she was a very hard worker: Clara once said that she "always did two days work in one." But when people did things her mother disliked, she would grow angry, mutter and curse. She often fed her family fruit that was getting rotten, and sometimes would make a batch of scrumptious pies and then not let the family eat them until they had gone bad.

*Clara Barton's mother was a difficult woman and argued with Clara's father a good deal. She was, nonetheless, a very hard worker and kept the household running well.*

*Clara's father was a stern, serious man, but he was kindly as well. Clara always had great love for him.*

Making matters worse, Clara's older sister Dolly suffered from insanity. In time she had to be kept locked in a room with bars over the windows. The family had to endure her howls and cries from the room above. Not all of the family were troubled. Clara adored her father, a sensible, hard-working man, and was close to her two brothers and other sister, who did well in their lives. But given the squabbling between her mother and father, it is not surprising that Clara grew up to be timid.

At the time Massachusetts, like much of America, was blanketed with farms, most of them owned and worked by single families. By the time of Clara's birth a few mills and factories were springing up here and there, especially in New England. But most people worked on farms, and Clara was no different.

Her family had been in Massachusetts for many generations. Some of her forebears had been doctors, lawyers, government officials. Her own father was at times a selectman of the town and a representative to the Massachusetts legislature. He bred fine horses, had some money, and was respected in North Oxford.

*Clara Barton was born on this very comfortable farm in North Oxford, Massachusetts. Her family was well-off for the time and owned mills and other farms. Clara enjoyed running loose in the countryside when her work was done.*

In those days, life was much harder than it is today. There were few machines of any kind. Clothes were washed by hand, heat came from wood-burning stoves, and the wood had to be sawed and split by hand. Hay was cut by scythes swung to a rhythm. People grew their own vegetables, slaughtered and cured their own beef and pork. Growing up, people learned that working hard, not having fun, was the most important thing.

*Farmers harvesting pumpkins in the fall. In the background are corn shocks, stalks of corn bundled together for later use as fodder for animals.*

Clara learned early to be serious about life, and she would always be. She was taught to cook, to sew, to weave cloth on hand looms, make soap and candles, and many other things.

She was not a pretty child, although by no means homely. "Plain" was the term used then. She had a lively face—"bright brown eyes and a heavy mop of dark brown hair." And she had a spunky, stubborn streak, despite her shyness, that would also last out her life. Energetic and active, she always wanted to be doing something. At the age of five her older brother David put her on a horse and showed her how to ride. She took to horses immediately, and became an excellent horsewoman. In those days it was considered unladylike for a girl to ride astride a horse as men did. Special "sidesaddles" were made for women, which allowed them to dangle both legs down the same side of the horse. Clara was made to ride sidesaddle, but she avoided sidesaddles as much as she could. She wanted to ride the way boys did.

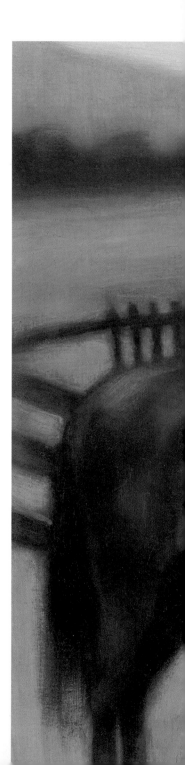

In fact, she wanted to do everything that boys did. Why shouldn't she? Among other things, it was not considered proper for girls to ice-skate. Clara was not allowed to, and she resented it. One time, when she noticed some of the boys she knew marching past to go skating on a nearby pond, she slipped out of the house and followed them. One of the boys lent her his skates. Very quickly she got the knack of it. Unfortunately, she fell, crashing onto some rough ice. Her knees were cut. She bandaged the wounds herself, and tried to conceal them from her parents, but of course they found out, and she was stopped from skating thereafter.

*Skating has been a popular sport for centuries. From the earliest days of American history, children have liked to skate on local ponds. However, Clara's parents thought that it was unladylike for girls to skate and would not let her do it.*

It was the same story with dancing. Dances of the time were more complicated than they are today and took practice. Clara learned that dancing classes were to be held nearby. Dancing was just the sort of energetic, exciting thing that Clara liked. She asked her parents to let her go to dancing class. They considered it and finally said no. Dancing was frivolous—not the kind of thing a properly brought-up girl ought to do.

But life was not always harsh. There were plenty of other children nearby with whom she could run in the fields, play in the woods, jump in haystacks. She never had any interest in dolls, but she loved animals, as she always would. She kept her own duck and learned to milk cows. She rode horses whenever she could—her father had plenty of them on their farms. Somebody gave her some canaries and she set them free. She had a dog named Button who slept with her. Shy she may have been; flying across a field on a horse, with the wind in her ears and her hair streaming out behind, nobody would have believed it.

Nor would they have believed it if they had seen how eagerly she listened to the stories of war her father told. One of her grandfathers had fought in the American Revolution, which had ended fifty years before. Her father had fought on the frontier against Indians under the famous general "Mad" Anthony Wayne. He told Clara about battling the Indians, about how soldiers drilled, about the way officers were ranked, with majors over captains and colonels over majors. He told about how tents were put up, guns loaded, cannon aimed. Clara enjoyed the stories. More importantly, they gave her an understanding of army life that would be a help to her when she had to deal with both ordinary soldiers and colonels and generals later in life.

And yet, despite this interest in soldiering, despite her love of riding, skating, her tomboyish ways, she remained a shy, sensitive child, always afraid to assert herself. To cure her of shyness her parents decided to send her away to boarding school. She didn't last. Lonely and homesick, she lost her appetite and stopped eating. Her family gave up the experiment and brought her home.

By this time her two brothers, David and Stephen, were grown up.

*Clara much admired her brother Stephen and may have picked up her tomboyish ways from him. Stephen was for periods a prosperous businessman, but like many of the Barton's, could sometimes be erratic.*

Unhappily, when they were helping to raise a barn, David fell from up near the roof and was seriously injured. In those days, as we shall see in more detail later, very little was known about the causes and cures of illnesses. It was commonly believed that many illnesses could be helped by drawing some blood from the patient. We know today that bloodletting only made the patient weaker. A lot of the medicines used at the time were actually poisonous and made patients even sicker than they had been.

Such cures were tried with David. He did not improve. Clara made it her job to nurse him through his illness. Nobody told her she had to: already, at the age of eleven, she felt that if somebody was suffering, she must do something about it. It was not the way most eleven-year-olds think; but Clara Barton was different.

*Clara's brother David in his Civil War army uniform. He served in the quartermaster corps, dealing with supplies. Clara nursed him back to health after a fall when she was not yet a teenager, a typical example of her willingness to sacrifice herself for others.*

David was in fact suffering a great deal. He was "sleepless, nervous, cold, dyspeptic—a mere wreck of his former self." Clara brought him food to tempt his appetite, gave him his medicines, learned to handle the worm-like leeches used to draw blood from him. For two years he remained sick. Clara would not give up. Doggedly she kept on nursing him, determined that he would grow better.

Then one day they heard about a new cure, which people were having good luck with. It was called *hydrotherapy*, meaning "water cure," and involved subjecting the patient to hot steam. It worked: David rapidly grew better and soon was back in good health. Today we realize that David came back to health because with hydrotherapy the bloodletting and dangerous medicines were stopped. But the experience of nursing him would prove invaluable to Clara later in life.

However, two years of being shut off from the world with David in a sick room had left her feeling shyer than ever. David tried to help. He taught Clara to throw like a boy, told her to be more positive and assertive. But the shyness remained. Her parents were very concerned. Soon she would be a grown-up. What was she going to do with her life? The usual thing for a young woman then was to marry, have children, and settle down to the hard job of managing a home.

Clara assumed she would follow that path. However, she had not yet met any young man she wanted to marry. There was no rush about that. Besides, she was more and more coming to believe that she had talents that ought to be expressed. What should she do?

Clara's mother talked to a man who knew Clara and whose opinion she respected. He said, "The sensitive nature will always remain. She will never assert herself for herself—she will suffer wrong first—but for others she will be perfectly fearless." Give Clara some responsibility, the man suggested. Why not make her a teacher? Both of her sisters and one of her brothers had tried their hands at teaching. And so it was decided.

# Chapter 2

# TRYING TO FIND HER WAY

IN 1839, WHEN CLARA BARTON BEGAN TO teach, public school systems like the ones we have today did not exist. In most cases schools were very small, often taught by people who knew little more than the students. The schools were not usually free; the parents had to pay. Many places had no schools at all. For example, Abraham Lincoln, growing up a generation before Clara, spent very little time in school; he taught himself mainly through reading whenever he could.

*This is the earliest known photograph of Clara Barton. It was probably taken when she was about thirty. The dogged determination that was at the center of her character shows in her face.*

But just around the time that Clara started teaching a man from Massachusetts named Horace Mann was developing the first real American public school system for his state. He was head of the Massachusetts board of education from 1837 to 1848. During this time, fifty new high schools were opened, teachers' salaries were raised, and new methods of teaching were worked out. Thus, just at the moment Clara became a teacher, education was booming. There would be plenty of jobs.

It was just as well, for teaching was one of the few careers open to women. Women—indeed girls—were allowed to work at the machines in the new mills being built everywhere. However, there was a lot of opinion against letting them get office jobs. Women could not become doctors or lawyers, could not go into the army or navy, could not become college professors, could not even go into business, unless it was some very small concern like running a pastry shop or selling their own eggs and cheese. By the time Clara began teaching, a few women were objecting to these ideas, and were trying to organize to fight back. But little progress had been made.

For a woman like Clara, who was smart and energetic, being fenced out of all the opportunities open to her brothers was very frustrating. David and Stephen could start a factory, go into politics, and when the time came, fight in war. Clara could do none of these things.

But at least she could teach. Despite the beginnings of a real school system being made by Horace Mann, schools of the time were small and rough. Most of them were the famous one-room schoolhouses that existed in many places in America well into the twentieth century. Some older people alive today can remember going to one-room schoolhouses.

*This picture of a typical one-room schoolhouse shows pupils taunting a newcomer. The painting is romanticized, but these schools could be rough. Clara Barton showed a marked ability to discipline unruly pupils like the ones shown here.*

Because most students, many of them quite small, walked to school, there had to be a lot of these one-room school-houses scattered around the countryside. In such schools, students of all ages, some as little as six, some as old as six-teen, were taught together. An eight-year-old might be ahead of a twelve-year-old in some subjects. Instead of teaching the whole class the same lesson, many times the teacher would have to go around the room teaching children on different levels as best she could.

The older students, especially the boys, were likely to be unruly. A big part of a teacher's job was keeping the students quiet. Teachers were allowed to hit, or even whip, students if they wanted to. Clara discovered the need for doing this very early. She had only begun teaching when an older boy, per-haps fifteen, challenged her authority. As it happened, Clara usually rode a horse to school, and she had with her in the classroom her riding whip. She picked it up and ordered the boy to do as he was told, or she would whip him.

"No you won't," he said.

Instantly she swung the riding whip, lashing him so hard he fell to the ground. Then, trembling with emotion, she dis-missed the class in order to pull herself together. She was standing there alone in the classroom when the boy she had whipped returned, carrying a bouquet of wildflowers he had picked for her. They became friends and he grew up to be a success as a man.

Through incidents like this one, Clara became known as a teacher who could control her students. As this was always a problem, she was in demand. One who knew her said, "She had such a happy way with her that she won everybody over to her side." She had no difficulty getting good teaching jobs. Her confidence in herself bloomed. Surprisingly, despite her ability to control her students, she grew close to many of them, who remembered her with fondness.

She "excelled in capturing not only the respect but the love of her pupils," one biographer said. Later she would run into many of them on the battlefield, some of them to die in her arms.

By 1850 Clara Barton had been teaching for more than ten years. She was almost thirty. She was a good, experienced teacher, much admired in the area by both students and school heads. But she felt that she ought to be doing more. She wanted, somehow, a larger task. But what?

She went back to school for awhile, and then in 1852 moved to New Jersey, where she had been offered a job. Here she saw boys with nothing to do but get into trouble. They ought to be in a school, she knew, but their parents couldn't afford to send them. She decided to open a free public school. She got backing and opened the first free school in New Jersey.

*The school in Bordentown, New Jersey, that Clara Barton started—the first free school in the state.*

So successful was the school that by 1854 she had six hundred students and a brand-new building that had cost four thousand dollars, a large amount of money at the time. But as ever, there remained prejudices against women in positions of power. It was decided to put a man over her. Angry and frustrated, she resigned.

What now? She was beginning to conclude that she would never marry. Several men had been interested in her, and she had been in love with one of them. That had not worked out; and Clara now believed that her life should be devoted to some kind of valuable work—although over her life several men wanted to marry her.

She decided, then, that she would move to Washington, D.C. She later said that she moved there because she had a sore throat and felt that the climate in Washington would be better for her. It sounds like an excuse: the climate of Washington is not ideal for sore throats. We are forced to suspect that Clara really went to Washington in order to find the large task she was seeking. It needs to be understood that Clara Barton, for all of her great virtues, sometimes exaggerated her deeds, or overdramatized the events she was in, which were often dramatic enough as it was. It is probable that the excuse she made for moving to Washington was to conceal her ambition to do great work: at the time, ambition was not considered nice in a woman.

At the moment Washington was certainly the place for larger tasks. As students of American history will know, when Clara arrived in Washington in 1854, tension between the Northern and Southern states was growing. The two sections of the country had always been rivals and had argued over many points. But more and more the contention was about slavery.

*The antislavery cause in the North was gathering force during the 1850s and earlier. This painting shows an antislavery meeting in 1840, in which an impassioned speaker is trying to rouse his audience to action against slavery.*

Northerners were by no means all opposed to slavery. Although slavery had been ended in the North some time before, many Northerners thought it was a problem for the South to deal with. Let Northerners stay out of it.

But a growing number of Northerners were coming to think that slavery was immoral and inhuman and ought not to be allowed in a democratic nation like the United States. In time the people who wanted to see slavery abolished would be a majority in the North.

This does not mean that all abolitionists wanted equality for African Americans: freedom, yes; equality, no. In fact, probably the majority of Northerners were not sure that blacks ought to be allowed to vote, to run for political office, or enjoy all the rights that whites had. Many did, of course, believe in equality for blacks, but a great many did not. However, by the time Clara reached Washington, the tide of opinion in the North was rising against slavery.

Needless to say, the more Northerners opposed slavery, the more Southerners grew determined to keep their slaves. The nation was headed for a showdown. In and out of government, people desperately sought compromises. At times such compromises were found. But then hotheads on one side or another would make more demands, and the compromises would break down.

This was the situation in the United States when Clara got to Washington. She had not come to teach. A little while later she was offered a teaching job. She replied, "I have out-grown all that, or that me. I dread the routine of such a life. I am to blame, I know, for nobody teaches so easily or has so little trouble with it."

To play a larger role, she decided to get a government job. This was not an easy thing to do. The prejudice against having women in offices existed in the government, too. However, not all men objected. As it happened, the man who ran the government Patent Office, Charles Mason, was willing to hire some women. Most of these women were copyists. At a time before copying machines and computers, everything had to be written out by hand. If a businessman or official wanted to keep a copy of a letter he had written, somebody had to copy it. Charles Mason used women copyists in his office.

*The Patent Office building in Washington, D.C., at the time Clara Barton worked there. It was unusual for women to work in the offices at that time, but the head of the Patent Office was more accepting of the idea than most officials were.*

Clara knew about this. However, she wanted to do more than simply copy letters. Because her family was prominent in central Massachusetts, they had influence with Massachusetts people in the Washington government. Through her connections, then, she was able to meet with Charles Mason. She impressed him, as she would impress many other people, as an intelligent, accomplished, energetic woman. He hired her to be his confidential secretary. Clara was now learning something that would be critically important to her success: how to get powerful men to back her up when she had a job she wanted to do.

A lot of the men in the Patent Office resented having a woman around. They spat tobacco near her, made jokes about her, blew cigar smoke in her face as if by accident. And of course they gossiped about her. But Clara was determined to stick it out, and she did.

Not everybody was pleased. President Franklin Pierce did not like seeing women in government offices. Neither did his secretary of the interior, who controlled the Patent Office. He said, "There is such an obvious impropriety in the mixing of sexes within the walls of a public office that I am determined to arrest the practice." For awhile Clara was able to hang onto the job, but in 1857 when President James Buchanan took over, she was fired. Very saddened, she went back to Oxford to rest. We see now another side to Clara Barton. Very often when she could not be active, could not be in the middle of things, she would become very dispirited and depressed. At times in her life she became so low in mind that she could barely get out of bed. She always came out of these low periods, but she would be quite miserable when she was in them.

This time her spirits picked up quickly, and she returned to Washington. Fortunately, there had been some changes in the Patent Office, and Clara got her job back.

She had arrived just at the moment when the nation was heading toward its greatest crisis. Many Southerners had concluded that the North meant to take away their slaves. They were determined it wouldn't happen. A lot of Southerners were now saying that the Southern states ought to split off from the United States, or Union as it was often termed. They would form their own government and do as they liked about their slaves. Not all Southerners wanted to secede, or separate, from the Union, by any means; perhaps even a majority were opposed to the idea. But those in favor were very fervent about their cause.

*The scene at Lincoln's inaugural address. In his speech, Lincoln tried to assure the South that he did not intend to end slavery where it already existed. Southerners did not believe him, and shortly afterward the Civil War began.*

In 1860 Abraham Lincoln was elected president. Although he personally opposed slavery, to him the crucial thing was to keep the Union whole. He told Southerners that if they would stay in the Union he would not try to end slavery where it already existed.

*A photograph of Abraham Lincoln, not long before he became president.*

Clara Barton was strongly against slavery, of course, but she did not really understand how determined Southerners were. In January 1861 she wrote a friend, saying, "Secession is wearing out in its infancy, and if wisely left alone, will die a natural death before its maturity." She couldn't have been more wrong. More and more Southern states seceded. Then, in April 1861 South Carolina attacked Fort Sumter, a Union stronghold on an island in Charleston harbor. The Union troops there were badly outgunned and had to surrender. The Civil War was on.

Four days later the Sixth Regiment from Massachusetts marched through Baltimore, Maryland, on their way to defend Washington in case of an attack by the new Confederate government of the South. Many Marylanders owned slaves and sympathized with the South. They attacked the Sixth Massachusetts Regiment men as they marched through, wounding thirty and killing three. Some of the regiment's men were from the area around Oxford. Some of them, she realized, had been her students.

The Sixth Massachusetts Regiment, one of the first groups to be called up to fight. When the regiment marched through Baltimore on its way to Washington, they were mobbed by Marylanders, many of whom supported the South. A number of Clara Barton's former pupils who were in the regiment were wounded.

When the regiment got to Washington the men were sheltered in the Senate chambers. As was her nature, Clara rushed over to give what help she could to the soldiers. The men were hungry, tired, sick, and in some cases seriously wounded. And there was really nobody to look after them. That may seem surprising, but in those days armies did not carry along with them a lot of doctors, nurses, and medical aides as they do today. Very often the wounded were left to suffer and die before anyone came around to help them.

Clara hastily rounded up what food, bandages, and comforts she could. She went among the Massachusetts men, feeding the hungry, treating the wounded, comforting the ill. Among the men she saw former students, who cheered, wept, and hugged her.

Clara quickly realized that she could not care for all these men by herself. She wrote letters to friends and to newspapers back home about the suffering men, and begged readers to send her supplies. There was a huge response. Packages of food, clothing, and bandages, poured in. There was so much of it that she had to rent space in a warehouse to store it all.

She knew now that here was the work she had been born to do. She wrote a friend that around her was the constant roll of military drums. "It is the music I sleep by, and I love it . . .

I may be compelled to face danger, but never fear it, and while our soldiers can stand and fight, I can stand and feed and nurse them." It was a statement to which she would live up.

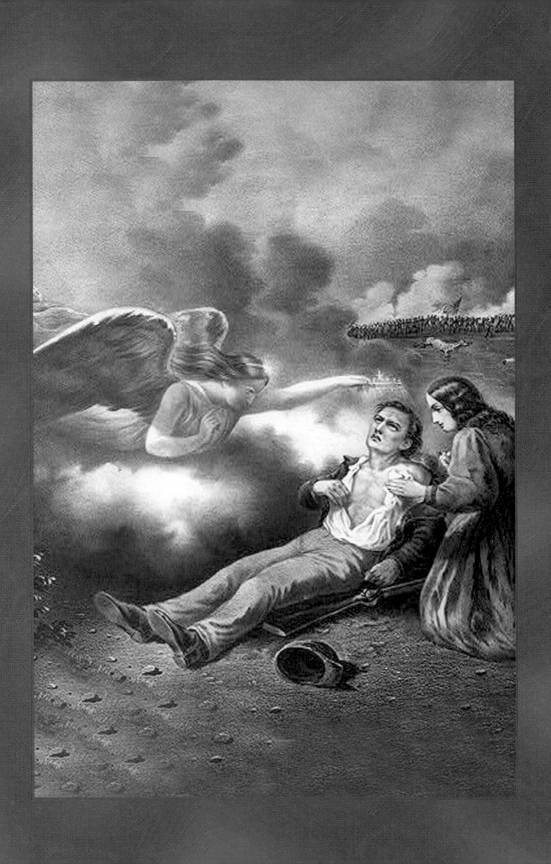

# Chapter 3

# THE ANGEL OF THE BATTLEFIELD

AT THE TIME THE CIVIL WAR BEGAN, modern medicine was still in its infancy. The idea that invisible creatures like bacteria and viruses caused a lot of diseases was not understood. Nor was it realized that keeping everything clean was crucial to preventing infections. Hospitals were often dirty. Doctors did not always wash their hands between operations. As a result, many people got sick and died from small wounds that could easily be cured today.

*Clara Barton and other women who volunteered to go onto the battlefield to help the wounded got a lot of publicity. They were sometimes called "angels of the battlefield." This highly romanticized picture shows one such woman being aided by an angel from heaven as she stanches blood from the chest of a wounded soldier.*

Nor was much known about anesthetics to prevent pain. Ether and chloroform were known about, but they were not always available to army doctors. As we have seen in the case of Clara's brother David, all sorts of quack medicines were being used that sometimes made people worse instead of better. By the time of the Civil War most doctors had come to realize that bloodletting was not a good idea. They knew how to set broken bones, and do a few other things. But they were helpless to cure most illnesses. In most cases they could only let nature take its course and hope for the best. The truth is that during the Civil War more soldiers died of diseases than from bullets and cannon shells. Diseases inevitably spread rapidly through large groups of men living closely together, drinking from the same cups and dippers, sharing bread and soup with dirty hands. Keeping the men healthy enough to fight was a constant problem for both armies.

There were always shortages of doctors, and the nursing profession had only just started. Not long before, an English woman named Florence Nightingale had pushed the idea of having women tend to wounded soldiers. As a result of her example, women began working in English hospitals as nurses. The work of Florence Nightingale was well known in America, and when the Civil War broke out, many women decided to do what she had done for English soldiers. Mainly because of pressure from women, an organization was formed, which came to he called "the Sanitary Commission."

It had the official job of taking care of sick and wounded soldiers. As the war went on, many women worked for the Sanitary Commission in army hospitals behind the lines. A lot of people were shocked by the idea of women going into hospitals where they were bound to see dreadful sights and hear much rough language. But these nurses saved the lives of thousands of soldiers.

*Florence Nightingale was an English woman who went into British army hospitals to aid British soldiers, and in so doing helped to found the profession of nursing. Her example inspired Clara Barton and other American women to do the same during the Civil War.*

Clara Baron could have joined the Sanitary Commission. With her natural ability to organize things, she soon would have had a prominent position in the organization. But that was not Clara's way. She was always a person who liked to do things herself, her own way. She liked to be able to go directly to where the problem was, rather than ask somebody higher up or meet with a committee first.

Very quickly she saw that she was going to be needed, for the war began disastrously for the Union armies of the North. That first summer, only three months after the attack on Fort Sumter that triggered the war, Union troops were badly beaten at the Battle of Bull Run, (sometimes called the Battle of Manassas), and fled in a panic back to Washington. Soon army hospitals were filled with wounded soldiers. Clara visited hospitals day after day, bringing food and whatever comforts she had. She had always been opposed to smoking and drinking. But soldiers wanted tobacco and whiskey, so she brought them.

Perhaps even more important, she was working out ways of getting the supplies she needed. She talked to people, wrote hundreds of letters, got stories in newspapers. All around the North, people, especially women, gathered together to collect supplies for the soldiers. They knit and sewed socks and blankets, made jelly and candies, cut and sewed vast quantities of bandages, collected medical supplies, canes, crutches. (Southern women were doing the same for their armies.) Not all of these supplies came to Clara; many were sent directly to the troops or went through other organizations. But Clara Barton was becoming well known to Americans. People trusted her to get supplies to where they were needed. Much of her work had to do with finding places to store these supplies.

She had come to realize that the situation in army hospitals was bad. There were never enough doctors and hardly any nurses, male or female. The food was often very bad. She knew, however, that as bad as things were in the hospitals, they were worse on the battlefields. The soldiers told her so. On the battlefield a soldier with a shattered leg might lie helpless and in agony for hours until somebody found him, sweating in the sun, shivering in the damp night chill. Thousands of men died who might have been saved had they been properly cared for. Clara wanted desperately to get to the battlefield.

The army, however, said no. The idea of women going onto a battlefield was strange, novel. Women then were thought of as delicate and in need of protection. It certainly seemed wrong to put them in danger.

But Clara was determined. She thought that what she was doing was right. What did it matter if she put herself in danger? Doggedly she persisted, seeking out men of authority who could help her. Again and again she was told no and turned away: a woman's place was not on the battlefield.

Then one day she decided to visit Major D. H. Rucker, who was assistant quartermaster general. An army quartermaster is responsible for getting supplies, from bullets to beef, and seeing that they are sent to the right places. And Clara had supplies.

Late one day she went to Major Rucker's office. "He was pressed and anxious," she wrote, "and I was very tired." As she waited, exhausted and dispirited by the rejections she had had, the tears began to flow. Or so she later said. But, in truth, Clara was learning that a flow of tears often got sympathy from men she had to deal with, when logic would not. To stop her crying Major Rucker took her back to his desk and asked her what she wanted. She told him that she wanted to go to the battlefield. That, he said, was no place for a woman. Why did she want to go there? Did she have relatives at the front? No, she told him, but she had a warehouse full of supplies—food, bandages, tobacco, medicines, and much else.

Major Rucker was startled. All these things were badly needed. Suddenly his manner changed. He issued an order that Clara was to have as many wagons as she needed and men to load them. "And here," he said, "is your permit to go to the front, and God bless you."

Thus began Clara Barton's career as the "angel of the battlefield," as the press soon started calling her. Wearing a dark skirt, a plaid jacket, and her brown hair tied up in a kerchief, she rode a four-mule wagon into Virginia two days after the bloody battle of Cedar Mountain. She arrived at the army hospital in nearby Culpepper just as doctors were running out of bandages, and burst in with a wagonload of them. She said later that by luck she always seemed to turn up somewhere just when she was needed.

Clara and some other women reached the battlefield when the guns were still firing. At a small railroad station hundreds of wounded and dying men lay on a thinly wooded hillside. A train was in the station taking on the wounded. Clara's women walked among them, handing out soup, beef, jellies, coffee. They bandaged wounds and then saw that the men were loaded onto the train. As she was moving among moaning soldiers she glanced down at a young man with a shattered arm. He was one of her former students. He threw his good arm around her and burst into tears. She tended to him and saw to it that he was put aboard the train.

Then, as night fell and it grew dark, someone told her of a dying man who kept crying out for his sister, Mary. Clara went to him, put her arms around him, and whispered that she was Mary. Again and again he thanked Mary for coming to him. But then dawn broke, and he saw that it was not his sister at all. Still, he thanked Clara for the comfort it had given him to think that his sister had been with him; and he died.

It rained, and she went among the soldiers putting dry socks on wet feet. Once she snatched a little sleep in a tent. As it rained, water drained through the tent. She awoke, soaked, and went on working. Then somebody shouted that Confederate troops were coming. Horsemen appeared at the top of the rise. Clara climbed aboard the train as it was pulling away. When she got back to Washington she slept in her own bed for twenty-four hours.

That was the kind of life Clara Barton would lead as the Civil War went endlessly on. Much of her time was taken up with sending out appeals for supplies, and organizing them as they poured in. She ran her warehouses, kept the records, did much of the work herself. But she spent as much time as she could on the battlefields.

One of the most important battles in the Civil War was at Antietam. The fighting that day was the bloodiest of the war. Almost 5,000 men died and over 18,000 were wounded in the course of a few hours. The North considered Antietam a victory, although it was a close victory. It emboldened Abraham Lincoln to issue the celebrated Emancipation Proclamation, which would eventually free the slaves.

Clara Barton knew in advance that the Antietam fight was coming up. She was determined to be in on it as soon as possible. She had a wagonload of supplies and four men to assist her. Although she ought to have been coming along after the troops, she got up at one o'clock in the morning, and caught up with the artillery. She reached the battlefield even before the ammunition wagons got there.

She ended up in the Union camp facing the rebels. She could see the battle unfold, the lines of men in the hills firing at each other. Even as the firing was going on, she moved her wagon forward to a house by the battlefield that doctors were using as a temporary hospital. When she got there she discovered that the doctors were almost out of bandages, and were using leaves from cornstalks instead. Hastily she unloaded the bandages from her wagon and gave them to the much-relieved doctors.

*Another very rough field hospital, set up in a cornfield. The wounded are protected from the sun and rain only by canvas roughly draped over wooden frames.*

She then got a fire going, filled a barrel with water, and began making a huge soup. Somebody who was there later described her "with sleeves rolled up to her elbows . . . with dress skirt turned up and that portion which should normally constitute the bottom pinned up around the waist . . . using a ladle to stir something like a barrel-full of soup . . ."

Even as the shooting continued, she went around the battlefield bringing soup, water, and bread to tired and hungry men, bandaging the wounded, consoling the dying. Once she stooped down to give a wounded man a drink of water. She put one hand behind his head to lift it so he could drink. Suddenly she felt something twitch the loose sleeve of her dress. The man she was holding jerked up and "fell back quivering in the agonies of death." A bullet had slashed through Clara's sleeve and into the man's chest, killing him as she held him.

As a result of the bravery, stamina, and resourcefulness Clara showed at Antietam, Bull Run, and other places, the Union army began to see the great value she had. It was not just the supplies she brought and the men she fed and bandaged; it was also, as the soldiers came to know about her, that the sight of her on a battlefield cheered them up. They knew that with Clara there they would have somebody to help them if they were wounded.

The soldiers' love for her was clear. During a bloody battle at Fredericksburg an official saw her, a lone woman, in the middle of the fighting. He raced up to her and said, "You are alone and in great danger, Madam. Do you want protection?" Clara answered, "I believe myself to be the best protected woman in the United States." A soldier standing nearby shouted at the official, "That's so." Suddenly the official realized who she was. "I believe you are right, Madam," he said.

Another time she was in Lincoln Hospital in Washington. In one ward all of the wounded men there had been tended by her on a battlefield. As she came in all of them saluted her, although some of them could not rise and saluted lying down. One famous general, Benjamin Butler, told his officers, "Honor any request that Miss Barton makes without question. She out-ranks me."

*The Armory Square Hospital in Washington, D.C. Soldiers who survived in the field hospitals were transferred to regular hospitals where they got better care. Barton often worked in such hospitals.*

By this time she had become nationally famous. There were many stories about her in newspapers. Thousands of soldiers wrote home to their families about seeing her while the bullets were flying or having been given a mug of soup by her.

But not everybody was on her side. Some of the top officials, especially ones connected to the Sanitary Commission, disliked the idea of the independent-minded Clara Barton coming and going among the troops as she liked. Besides, she was getting a lot more publicity than others who were also doing good work. The publicity was not Clara's fault, of course—to newspapers she was a good story. But it annoyed others, nonetheless. The result was that she found it harder and harder to get permission to go onto the battlefield. Soon her battlefield trips ended. But throughout the dreadful Civil War she continued to work in hospitals, bringing food, treats, writing letters home for soldiers, simply comforting them in their pain.

The war seemed to go on and on. In towns and villages in both the North and South legless and armless young men sat uselessly on town benches.

Then, in March 1864, General Ulysses S. Grant took over the Northern armies. He was a tough soldier. Lincoln said, "I can't spare this man. He fights." Northerners were cheered up by the arrival of Grant in Washington, none more so than Clara Barton.

Gradually the North began to win. By the time that the Civil War ended, Clara Barton was better known to Americans than many of the generals who had commanded during the war.

# Chapter 4

# LOOKING FOR A NEW LIFE

THE YEARS FOLLOWING THE CIVIL WAR were not good ones for Clara Barton. She was famous, that was true: one of her biographers said, "Children gazed at her with wonder. Her name became a household word. A national heroine was in the making." She went on speaking tours, even though standing up in front of an audience made her very nervous. "I am the most timid person on earth," she said. "All speech-making terrifies me." When she was lecturing she seemed to her audiences very calm, even stately. But inside she was filled with butterflies.

*This formal portrait of Clara Barton, taken in the famous Mathew Brady studio, is probably the best-known picture of her. It was taken about 1865.*

She was also, for the first time in her life, financially comfortable. She was never rich, and really didn't much care to be. But between her earnings from lecturing and some investments she had made, she had enough money to allow her to do what she wanted.

But once again, what did she want to do? She knew she must be active to be happy and in good spirits, and she knew she had to work at something that was mainly for the good of others. First she decided to help identify dead soldiers buried in unmarked graves. In battle, the names of many who die are lost, so young men are buried with just a cross over them, without a name on it. Their parents, children, and wives know that they must be dead, but have no idea where or when they died. They usually want to find out, so they can put a marker on the grave.

At the end of the Civil War over a hundred thousand Union soldiers had been buried in unmarked graves. Clara wangled a meeting with President Lincoln and asked—indeed insisted—that she be allowed to work on helping to identify soldiers missing in action—MIAs we call them today.

Lincoln agreed that she could do it, and for a time the MIA work occupied her. And because of her fame, there were other causes people tried to interest her in. One of these was what we today call *feminism*, which at the time was termed the *woman movement*. We have seen clearly enough in Clara's story that many doors were closed to women. They were not welcomed in most business and government offices, could not go into the professions, were not permitted on the battlefield even when dying men were crying for help.

More, perhaps, than any woman of her time, Clara Barton had bulled her way over, around, and through such obstacles. She had managed to keep her job in the Patent Office when no less than the president wanted her out, managed to get onto the battlefield, managed to get onto the MIA committee. She had gone on lecture tours, had worked with many men at high levels in government. She was a great example of what a woman could accomplish when she set her heart and mind to it.

Inevitably, many of the feminist leaders of her time wanted her to join their organizations. They wanted to use her enormous prestige to demand greater freedom and opportunities for women. Clara was very sympathetic to the woman movement. She knew well from her own experience how difficult it was for women to break through the barriers men had set up around them. She was all for greater rights for women.

I was strong – and I thought I ought to go to the rescue of the men who fell –:

But I struggled long and hard with my sense of propriety – with the appalling fact – that I was only a woman, whispering in one ear – and the groans of suffering men, dying like dogs – unfed and unsheltered, for the life of the very Institutions which had protected and educated me – thundering in the other –

I said that I struggled with my sense of propriety – and I say it with humiliation and shame – Before God and Before you I am ashamed that I thought of such a thing –

But when our armies fought a Cedar Mountain I Broke the shackles and went to the field

Notes Clara Barton made for one of her many speeches about her life and work. Here she discusses the internal struggle she had between her wish to help wounded men and her fear that going into hospitals and onto battlefields would be seen as "improper" for a woman. Of course, in the end she went where she was needed, regardless of what people thought.

But she had some cautions about the woman movement, too. For one thing, she had reached her goals not by opposing men, but by getting them on her side. She had become very clever at arranging to meet important people—even presidents. Not every important man liked her; many thought she was too bold for a woman. But many men appreciated her direct, forthright way of doing things. She did not shout, or raise her voice. She always had good arguments for what she wanted. She was persistent. Her way was not to fight men, but to bring them around to her side.

For a second thing, Clara Barton had always been an independent-minded woman who liked running her own show, liked doing things the way she thought best. She did not like to work in big organizations—the Sanitary Commission was one example—where she had to go by the rules, follow set procedures. Instead, she always wanted to shoot directly ahead in the way she thought best to help others. So although she strongly sympathized with the woman movement and was good friends with some of the leaders, like Susan B. Anthony, Lucy Stone, and Frances Willard, she never made the movement her main cause.

However, she needed something to do, and when the MIA work was finished, she had no occupation. As ever, her spirits drooped. Nothing she did seemed to help. Then one day, when she was giving a lecture, she suddenly stopped speaking. She could not go on and walked off the speaker's platform.

For several years thereafter her spirits rolled up and down. Sometimes she would be able to work at tasks she liked. Other times she would feel so depressed that she would go to bed and stay there for days, feeling too bad to do anything.

The first tiny beginning of a new life for Clara came in 1869, four years after the Civil War had ended. She was still depressed, her spirits low. She hoped that travel would cheer her up. She decided to go to Europe for awhile. She was tired. "How time flies," she wrote, "and how little do I accomplish. I must believe my life an entire failure."

So she went. And on this trip she heard for the first time about the Geneva Convention and an organization that had sprung out of it—the Red Cross. The story of the Red Cross begins with a youth from Geneva, a major city in Switzerland, which has often been headquarters for international organizations. The youth's name was Jean Henri Dunant. He worked his way up in banking and made a good deal of money.

In 1859, just as the United States was plunging toward the Civil War, Dunant made a business trip to a place in Italy near Solferino. A terrible battle had just been fought there. Dunant came upon it while the dead and wounded were still scattered in heaps around the battlefield. He was stunned, shocked. He plunged in among the wounded, just as Clara would do three years later. He used his own money to buy medical supplies. He rounded up volunteers to help the wounded. He himself bandaged helpless men.

Seeing so much pain and death was a powerful experience for Dunant. It affected him deeply—so much so that it changed his life. He was particularly struck by the way the wounded were left cruelly unattended, to suffer for hours, or even days, and frequently to die when with help they might have lived. In 1862 he wrote a book about the cruel treatment of the wounded in war. In the book he talked a great deal about what Florence Nightingale had done for British soldiers during their wars.

Dunant's book awoke many people to the need to aid wounded soldiers. Among them was another man from Geneva, Gustave Moynier. Together, Dunant and Moynier got both the European public and many heads of state to support the idea of an organization devoted to the care of the wounded. And in 1863, sixteen nations sent delegates to a conference to discuss the idea. There was great enthusiasm for it. On August 22, 1864, a group of nations signed what has been known ever since as the Geneva Convention. It gave birth to the organization today known as the Red Cross. This organization was to be neutral— it would belong to no nation, but would help the wounded from all sides who fell in battle.

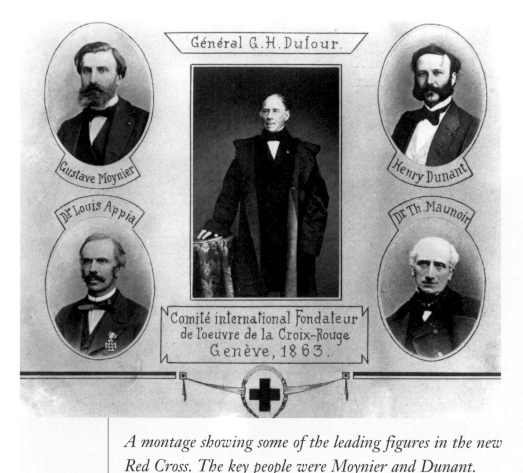

*A montage showing some of the leading figures in the new Red Cross. The key people were Moynier and Dunant.*

However, one major nation did not sign the Geneva Convention: the United States. When Clara Barton learned about the Geneva Convention and the Red Cross, she was stunned. It seemed impossible that she had never heard of it, but she hadn't. What had happened?

*The Red Cross at work during one of Europe's many small wars in the nineteenth century, this time in 1866. The Red Cross was up and running in Europe at a time when few Americans had ever heard of it, a situation Clara Barton hoped to change.*

In fact, the American government had been urged by Dunant and others to send delegates to the Geneva Convention. The leaders very much wanted the United States to join, especially as the nation was just then in the midst of a bloody war. But William Seward, secretary of state to Abraham Lincoln, refused to send anyone to Geneva.

At the time there seemed to be good reasons for this decision. For one, the government was busy fighting the Civil War and could not think about much else. Perhaps more important, Americans had long been suspicious of Europe. Nations there seemed to be undemocratic, which was largely true. They also seemed not to live by ideals, but were always signing treaties and breaking them when it was in their interest to do so. This opinion of Europe was somewhat unfair: Americans did not always live by their ideals either. But there was enough truth in it to convince many Americans that the less they had to do with Europe the better. The United States had its Sanitary Commission, its army hospitals; it would take care of its own sick and wounded. So Seward had said no to the forming of a Red Cross organization in America.

But Clara Barton instantly saw the value of the new Red Cross: she had seen the misery of the battlefield herself. As ever, when she made up her mind about something, she was not troubled by the opinions of presidents and kings.

Then, by chance, she was drawn onto a European battlefield. In 1870 a war broke out between Germany and France, known today as the Franco-Prussian War. Clara fell in with a handsome young Swiss woman named Antoinette Margot, who spoke several European languages and could translate for Clara and help in other ways. Clara got them assigned to the Red Cross, and they set off, carrying a Red Cross insignia. All armies were supposed to respect the Red Cross and allow their workers to go into hospitals and onto battlefields.

*A portrait of a Red Cross nurse painted in 1886. By this time, the Red Cross was well known to Americans.*

But it did not always work. Once Clara and Antoinette left their Red Cross insignia behind on a bus. Clara was wearing a red bow—she had always been fond of the color red. She quickly took off the bow, fashioned a cross from it, and sewed it to her sleeve. Despite this, when she got to the area of the fighting, a German soldier discovered Clara and Antoinette in a tumble-down house where they had sought shelter. He put a sword to Clara's chest and threatened to kill her. She stared at him until he backed away.

She then reached the city of Strasbourg, France, which had been terribly damaged in the fighting. It was "a smoking shambles" where half-naked children "whimpered in damp cellars." Clara went to work organizing the local women to sew clothes from cloth she provided. She was back at work again.

In 1873 she was back in the United States. For a period she continued to suffer from the usual poor spirits, to the point where she had trouble working. But then war broke out between Russia and Turkey in 1877. The fighting made the importance of the Red Cross clear. Clara decided to fight for an American branch. She was the Clara Barton of old.

# Chapter 5

# FOUNDING THE AMERICAN RED CROSS

THE FIRST JOB, CLARA DECIDED, WAS TO see if they could get the American government to ratify the Geneva Convention. That was going to take work. Even by this time few Americans had heard of the Red Cross. There was no public outcry to join.

By now Clara had had much experience in the ways of Washington. She knew how to get to important people. Through her contacts she arranged a meeting in the White House with President Rutherford B. Hayes. She told him about the Red Cross and the value it could have for the United

*A poster for the American Red Cross used during the terrible World War I of 1914–1918. The Americans did not enter the war until 1917. The Red Cross was very active during the fighting.*

States. President Hayes was conservative in his opinions, and was not enthusiastic about the idea. He sent her to his secretary of state. He would not even see Clara Barton, but sent her along to his assistant, Frederick W. Seward. He was the son of the older Seward who had refused to send delegates to the Geneva Convention. He, too, said no. "It is all settled; the question will never again be considered," he said.

Clara now realized she could not—at that time at least—expect any help from the United States government. That made her only more determined. She would build the organization herself, by getting donations from the public and wealthy people.

She further realized that she should change the direction of the organization. The Red Cross had been founded by Dunant after his experience on the battlefield of Solferino, and it was meant basically to care for war wounded. Europe, at the time made up of well over twenty squabbling nations, was likely to have wars break out regularly, as in fact they have right until today. The United States was one solid country, which rarely had problems with its immediate neighbors. There might not be wounded, at least at home, to care for.

However, the United States was certain to be hit again and again by natural disasters, as it always had been—floods, forest fires, hurricanes, earthquakes, tornadoes, drought. The government was really not set up to care for victims of such horrors.

Clara began publicizing the Red Cross. She wrote endless letters, talked to everybody she could. Then, in 1881, she got a break when James Garfield became president. Garfield had fought in several important battles in the Civil War and knew the problems of the wounded from experience. He had been a congressman for many years before being elected president. Clara had known him, and like other former soldiers, he was well aware of the work she had done with the wounded. Clara felt that Garfield might be sympathetic to the idea of the Red Cross.

She was now quite competent at meeting presidents and arranged to meet Garfield. As a man who had seen the agony of the wounded, he was interested. He told his secretaries of state and war to meet with her. Both of these men also liked the idea of the Red Cross. And on May 21, 1881, she held the first meeting of the American Red Cross.

But although the president and his cabinet ministers supported the idea, it would not be official until the Senate ratified the Geneva Convention. Clara knew she must get a lot of support from the public before the Senate would approve. She then began a publicity campaign to make the public aware of the Red Cross. She published a pamphlet about it and wrote many letters to newspapers and influential people. Although she had the backing and cooperation of the International Red Cross, the organization that Dunant and Moynier had built, Clara was basically spending her own money to get the United States to sign the Geneva Convention. Day after day she worked away, arguing, cajoling, persuading people, especially in the government. And in March 1882 all the work paid off. The Senate ratified the Convention, and the United States was finally part of the Red Cross. Clara Barton had accomplished this task against all odds almost entirely by herself.

Now she had to build an organization. As usual, she intended to oversee everything herself. This idea, that she must look after things herself, had its good and its bad points. On the good side, with her great energy, intelligence, and experience, she often got things done quicker and cheaper than an organized system would do. When she went to the scene of a disaster she would very rapidly see what needed to be done and get people moving within hours, if not minutes.

*A picture of Clara Barton during the years she was busiest developing the American Red Cross.*

But keeping all control in her own hands had its drawbacks, too. Money that came in and went out was not always properly marked down in account books. Clara sometimes ignored people who felt they ought to be consulted about this or that if she thought they were only getting in the way. And many of her coworkers resented Clara's idea that she knew what was best, although they often had to admit it was true. And finally, she far preferred to be out in the field, dealing with the victims of floods, forest fires, or hurricanes, than sitting in an office in Washington building a solid organization. The American Red Cross in Clara Barton's time never got much overall direction from the top.

Typical was a trip she made during a terrible flood of the Ohio and Mississippi Rivers in 1884. Clara was, we must remember, by now over sixty, an age at which many people think of slowing down, if not retiring altogether. Instead of sending younger people out to view the flood, she went herself. Quickly she appealed to the public for money. Some children decided to put on a little show to raise money, and sent Clara a check for $51.25—a good deal more money then than it is today.

Clara saw this as a chance to get some good publicity for the Red Cross. She looked around for a flood victim who really needed the money. She found a Mrs. Plew who had lost her home in the flood and was living with six children in a corncrib. Clara slogged through mud and rain to reach the Plews.

She wrote, "There was misfortune, poverty, sorrow, want and loneliness, dread of future, but fortitude, courage, integrity and honest thrift." She gave the Plews the money and helped them to get back on their feet. The story was just what the newspapers wanted.

So it went. During the terrible Johnstown flood of 1889 some three to four thousand people drowned, and the town was smashed to pieces. One husband and wife clung to each other's hands across the ridge pole of their house to keep from dropping into the raging water as their house was driven along. The Red Cross built a hotel, warehouses, and apartments for the flood victims. Four years later, in a hurricane that hit the Sea Islands of South Carolina, one thousand people were killed. Some victims climbed trees, and then the trees were blown into the sea. Clara spent months in the devastated area, sleeping on a cot and using a crate for her desk. She not only aided the victims, but brought in seeds to replant gardens, had ditches dug to drain flooded land, fences built, and in general left the area better than it had been before the flood. By now very experienced in helping victims, she understood that it was not enough just to hand money around; the important thing was to see that the victims were put back on their feet again, so they could rebuild their lives.

*The Johnstown Flood of 1889 was one of the worst disasters to hit the United States during the nineteenth century. The Red Cross, under Barton's direction, did incredible work to bring the town back to life.*

But her great success in the field was not helping the Red Cross to grow as many people thought it should. Indeed, some well-organized branches, like the New York branch, were growing rich and powerful, and generally did what they wanted without consulting Clara's national headquarters in Washington. People who ran the New York branch thought that the Red Cross ought to be run by a professional staff. Among other things, they believed that Clara Barton was getting too old to do the job. One critic said, "For thirteen years . . . the National Red Cross Association has been Miss Clara Barton, and Miss Clara Barton has been the National Red Cross Association." In particular, complaints were raised that Clara had always kept the financial records in her own hands. Nobody accused her of spending Red Cross money on herself; but how could people be sure she was spending the money wisely?

By the 1890s, when Clara was well in her seventies, pressure was growing for her to resign. She fought back. She had many supporters and clung to her office. She could fairly say that she had given birth to the American Red Cross and she did not want to give her baby up.

But in truth, her enemies were at least partly right. The American Red Cross had grown too big to be run by a single, elderly woman from her home. An ambitious, tough-minded woman named Mabel T. Boardman, who was wealthy and knew many important people, was especially determined to get Clara to resign. Still Clara tried to hang on. Finally, in 1904, when Clara Barton was in her eighties, she resigned from the Red Cross. It was "the saddest moment of her life." Her baby was gone from her. But she faced the loss with courage.

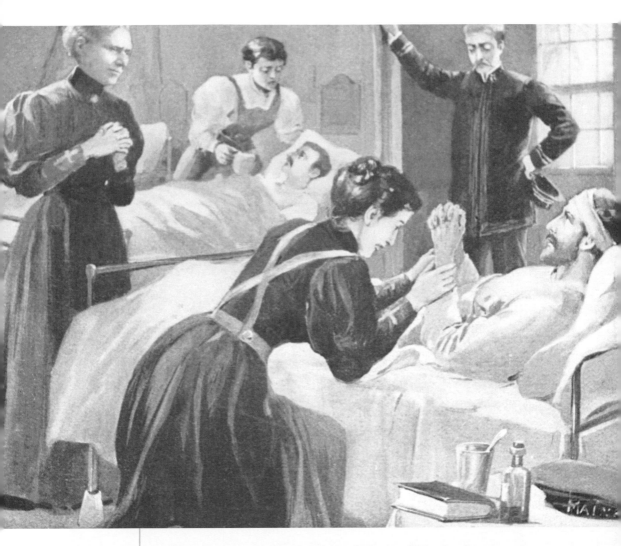

When the Spanish-American War in Cuba broke out
in 1898, Clara Barton responded like an old fire horse
hearing an alarm. She went herself to Cuba to tend the
wounded, even though many said she ought to remain in the
Washington headquarters to oversee things there. However,
she could not resist being in the thick of the action once
again. In this picture, she is standing at the foot of a
wounded man's bed, supervising Red Cross nurses.

Incredibly, she found another task to do. The idea of "first aid" had been growing. Too many people injured in war, accident, natural disaster, suffered and died because those around them did not know what needed to be done. The point of the First Aid Movement was to teach people how to save lives in the first moment after an accident. Clara, even as she was approaching ninety, took up this work, often spending her own money to keep the organization growing. Today first aid is taught everywhere to young Americans and has saved countless lives. Clara Barton played a major role in bringing the idea to Americans.

*Even after Clara Barton left the Red Cross she continued to be active in public life. Here, she attends a ceremonial tree planting.*

Clara Barton lived into her nineties. She continued to write hundreds of letters, to give interviews to newspapers, to keep an eye on how the Red Cross was doing. The organization was no longer hers, but she could look back on a long life of sacrifice and service to humankind that few people have equaled. Toward the end she wrote:

> *What armies and how much of war I have seen, what thousands of marching troops, what fields of slain, what prisons, what hospitals, what ruins, what cities in ashes, what hunger and nakedness, what orphanages, what widowhood, what wrongs and what vengeance. And yet one lives and laughs as if nothing had happened and thanks good fortune that it is as well as it is.*

On Good Friday, April 12, 1912, Clara Barton died. Her body was sent north to be buried in her hometown of North Oxford. As it was being carried in a wagon across New York City to the train that was to take her home, the driver of the wagon suddenly learned who was in the coffin. His mouth dropped open. His father had been shot in the neck during the Civil War. Clara Barton had bandaged the wound and saved his life.

As is clear from this map, the Civil War was fought in a lot of places many hundreds of miles apart. Two of the key battles, which led to Union victories on two consecutive days, were fought at Vicksburg and Gettysburg, cities a thousand miles from each other.

# Author's Note on Sources

Two recent books on the subject are *Clara Barton: Professional Angel*, by Elizabeth Brown Pryor, and *A Woman of Valor: Clara Barton and the Civil War*, by Stephen B. Oates. For students, there is her own *The Story of My Childhood*, which, however, may not be easily available. There is also *Clara Barton: Founder of the American Red Cross* in the American Women of Achievement series and Illustrious Americans: Clara Barton, by Marshall W. Fishwick.

Fishwick, Marshall W. *Illustrious Americans: Clara Barton*. Morristown, NJ: Silver Burdett, 1966. (young readers)

Leni, Hamilton. *Clara Barton: Founder of the American Red Cross*. New York: Chelsea House Publishers, 1988. (young readers)

Oates, Stephen B. *A Woman of Valor: Clara Barton and the Civil War*. New York: Macmillan, 1994.

Pryor, Elizabeth Brown. *Clara Barton: Professional Angel*. University of Pennsylvania Press: Philadelphia, PA, 1987.

# INDEX

American Red Cross, 6, *64*, 65–72
Anthony, Susan B., 55
Antietam, 45

Barton, David (brother), 10, 14–15, *15*, 16, 20
Barton, Dolly (sister), 7
Barton, Stephen (brother), 14, *14*, 20
battlefields, 41–47, 60
bloodletting, 15
Boardman, Mabel T., 72
Bordentown, New Jersey, 24, *24*
Buchanan, James, 29
Bull Run, 40, 47
Butler, Benjamin, 48

Childhood, 5–17
Civil War, 32–49

Death, 75
Dunant, Jean Henri, 56–57, *58*, 66, 67

Feminism, 53
First Aid Movement, 74
former students, 24, 33–34, 44
Franco-Prussian War, 60
Fredericksburg, 47

Garfield, James, 67
Geneva Convention, 56–59, 65–68
Grant, Ulysses S., 49

Hayes, Rutherford B., 65–66
hospitals, 37–40, 48–49
hydrotherapy, 16

Johnston flood of 1889, 70, *71*

Lecturing, 51–52, 55
Lincoln, Abraham, 31, *31*, 45, 49, 52, 59

Mann, Horace, 20, 21
Margot, Antoinette, 60, 62
Mason, Charles, 28–29

MIA (missing in action),
52–53, 55
Moynier, Gustave, 57, *58*, 67

Natural disasters, 66, 68–70,
74
Nightingale, Florence, 38,
*39*, 57
North Oxford,
Massachusetts, 6, *8*, 75
nursing, 38–39

One-room schoolhouse,
21–22
opposition and criticism, 25,
29, 41, 49, 55, 72

Parents, 6–7, *7*, 13–14, 17
Patent Office, 28–30, 53
personal traits, 7, 10, 14, 16,
20, 29, 30, 40, 41, 42, 46, 55,
56, 62, 68–69
photographs/portraits of
Clara Barton, *4*, *11*, *18*, *23*,
*34*, *43*, *50*, *63*, 68, *73*, *74*
Pierce, Franklin, 29

Red Cross, 56–63. *See also*
American Red Cross
Rucker, D.H., 42

Sanitary Commission, 39,
49, 60
Seward, Frederick W., 66
Seward, William, 59
Sixth Massachusetts
Regiment, 32, *33*
slavery, 26–27, 30–32
soldiers' respect for Clara
Barton, 47–48
Spanish-American War, *73*
Stone, Lucy, 55

Teaching, 19–25

Wayne, "Mad" Anthony, 13
Willard, Frances, 55
woman movement, 53, 55
words of Clara Barton, 28,
32, 34–35, 42, *54*, 56, 70, 75

# ABOUT THE AUTHOR

James Lincoln Collier has written many books, both fiction and nonfiction, for children and adults. His interests span history, biography, and historical fiction. He is an authority on the history of jazz and performs weekly on the trombone in New York City.

*My Brother Sam Is Dead* was named a Newbery Honor Book and a Jane Addams Honor Book and was a finalist for a National Book Award. *Jump Ship to Freedom* and *War Comes to Willy Freemen* were each named a notable Children's Trade Book in the Field of Social Studies by the National Council for Social Studies and the Children's Book Council. Collier received the Christopher Award for *Decision in Philadelphia: The Constitutional Convention of 1787*. He lives in Pawling, New York.